YOUR KNOWLEDGE HAS VALUE

- We will publish your bachelor's and master's thesis, essays and papers

- Your own eBook and book - sold worldwide in all relevant shops

- Earn money with each sale

Upload your text at www.GRIN.com and publish for free

Bibliographic information published by the German National Library:

The German National Library lists this publication in the National Bibliography; detailed bibliographic data are available on the Internet at http://dnb.dnb.de .

This book is copyright material and must not be copied, reproduced, transferred, distributed, leased, licensed or publicly performed or used in any way except as specifically permitted in writing by the publishers, as allowed under the terms and conditions under which it was purchased or as strictly permitted by applicable copyright law. Any unauthorized distribution or use of this text may be a direct infringement of the author s and publisher s rights and those responsible may be liable in law accordingly.

Imprint:

Copyright © 2015 GRIN Verlag, Open Publishing GmbH
Print and binding: Books on Demand GmbH, Norderstedt Germany
ISBN: 9783668235779

This book at GRIN:

http://www.grin.com/en/e-book/323684/book-review-of-the-five-dysfunctions-of-a-team-by-patrick-lencioni

Larry Peaden

Book Review of "The Five Dysfunctions of a Team" by Patrick Lencioni

GRIN Publishing

GRIN - Your knowledge has value

Since its foundation in 1998, GRIN has specialized in publishing academic texts by students, college teachers and other academics as e-book and printed book. The website www.grin.com is an ideal platform for presenting term papers, final papers, scientific essays, dissertations and specialist books.

Visit us on the internet:

http://www.grin.com/

http://www.facebook.com/grincom

http://www.twitter.com/grin_com

Book Review: Patrick Lencioni's (2002) The Five Dysfunctions of a Team, a Leadership Fable

PLACE OF PUBLICICATION: San Francisco, CA
PUBLISHER: Joessey-Bass
NUMBER OF PAGES: 228
ISBN: 978-0-7879-6075-9

Larry M. Peaden
Ed.D. Student, University of South Carolina
MSA School Administration, East Carolina University
BS Elementary Education, East Carolina University

Abstract

The Five Dysfunctions of a Team: A Leadership Fable by Patrick Lencioni is a realistic fictional story that focuses on a real-world scenario focused on the importance of team building skills. In the story, a relatively young, yet successful company recruited a new CEO. Recently the company was falling into decline, apparently by the dysfunctions of the executive team. The story followed the CEO in her efforts to unite the team in an attempt to encourage increased productivity and most importantly, an understanding of how a team should function. This review will examine the way one might apply the suggested techniques to a real-life situation.

Lencioni describes a realistic group of people who are not working together as a successful team. With Katheryn, the team's newly hired leader, the group explores and confronts the issues that are preventing them from being a successful team. The tense, realistic scenarios create a very interesting and entertaining text for the reader. However, the situations present useful techniques and skills that a leader could apply to real-life situations. The situations focus around business situations set in corporate America. The narrative text allows readers to envision the techniques in action; this book could benefit a leader who wants to acquire a few useful leadership skills while reading a relatively entertaining story.

Book Review: Patrick Lencioni's (2002) The Five Dysfunctions of a Team, a Leadership Fable

    Many people experience having to work with people from various backgrounds; many have found that they have difficulty creating successful, well-functioning teams with many people for a wide variety of reasons. One must ask what impact this difficulty creates for the greater good of an organization. What are the benefits of working as a team? What is the impact of choosing to work alone? What would one use to evaluate the pros and cons of a particular team? In *The Five Dysfunctions of a Team, a Leadership Fable*, Patrick Lencioni describes the foundation of a successful team and discusses ways to address these issues.

    The author, Patrick Lencioni is a consultant who specializes in building strong collaborative teams through a variety of organizations. Patrick Lencioni has worked with many Fortune 500 companies as well as other prominent organizations. He has written eight nationally recognized books that focus on team development and organizational health. Lencioni is often referenced by popular news media for his knowledge of business management.

    Lencioni argues that a team that does not function properly will snowball overtime into a disastrous situation. Lencioni mentions that a team must be aware of what a team must do to function well and collaborate in a manner that will lead to higher success with all members working toward a common goal. Throughout the book, the author reminds the reader that true team building is a process that involves work and effort over a long period. He also reminds the reader that in many instances there will be regression as deliberate team building is in the implementation process.

Summary of Contents

The Five Dysfunctions of a Team, a Leadership Fable follows Kathryn, the newly hired CEO of a fictional company called DecisionTech. DecisionTech is a relatively new company that experienced great initial success, but has failed to grow to its expectations. Kathryn inherited an executive team that processed a wide range of skills, extremely competent in their abilities to perform in their assigned position, but have disparate personalities. In addition to these varied personalities, team members also lack the ability to function as a team.

Kathryn sees creating a strong, functional team as her first and most important goal before any business related results can be obtained. Kathryn schedules a series of team-building retreats in order to strengthen her team. Throughout the book, Kathryn has to battle criticism, lack of cooperation, along with numerous other obstacles. The book reminds the reader why it is important for Kathryn to maintain the importance of her vision while remaining sensitive to the needs of the members of her executive team. There are numerous instances where Kathryn must be firm in emphasizing the importance and relevance of what the team is trying to accomplish with their meetings.

Lencioni describes "the five dysfunctions of a team" that hinder the capacity of the team to operate as a whole. These dysfunctions are simple, yet essential to understand: absence of trust, fear of conflict, lack of commitment, avoidance of accountability, and inattention to results. The book describes what these dysfunctions look like among this fictional team and describes what would need to occur in order to reshape these things into something positive. Throughout the story, there are sobering reminders that it is possible to experience a downfall both in the initial phases as well as during the rebuilding phases of a team that individuals simply are not a good-fit for a particular team regardless of their capabilities and skills.

Review of Content

In *The Five Dysfunctions of a Team, a Leadership Fable*, Lencioni does an exceptional job in creating a realistic story that illustrate the dysfunctions of a team. The book breaks the process up into sections and explains what the team is doing that creates the dysfunction and then creates narrative among the characters to discuss what could be done to fix the problems as well as potential implications of not fixing the problems. The fictional characters and setting provide the reader with a strong image of how these dysfunctions would look in a real-world situation. The narrative format also exposes the reader to the inner thoughts of the participants in this situation by discussing issues such as loyalty to your peers, feelings of discomfort in tense situations, and the importance of nurturing respect among colleagues. The various personalities among the characters also allow the reader to experience the ways in which certain people may react to various factors.

Due to the fact that the story is fictional, the reader is able to follow the development of the team throughout time. There is a flowing storyline with consistent characters that develop throughout the story. Lencioni describes characters who experience great break-throughs during the process of building a team. Readers are able to predict how one type of personality may respond to something compared to others; the characters ranged from executives who were extremely receptive to developing their team skills to people who eventually leave the company due to their uncompromising nature.

DecisionTech, the fictional company in the story is a technology business in California, but the dialogue among characters sets the narrative in such a way that one can easily envision how these types of trainings would work in other industries. The varying personalities of the characters allow the reader to infer how certain reactions may come up based upon the specific circumstances. It becomes clear that the author has worked closely with diverse teams throughout his career as an organizational health consultant and team-building keynote speaker.

One could easily apply many of the discussed tactics to a wide variety of teams. There are many things that Lencioni addresses that are essential for humans to get along well with others: trust, safety, common goals, etc. It seems that the author selected personalities that many may conceive as difficult to work with in order to allow the reader to imagine how tactics may work with real-life individuals.

While Lencioni presented many valid points on the importance of building a strong team, it is unclear how these practices may work within other teams. Lencioni may present a certain level of bias because the majority of his work involves working with prominent organizations. In the story, all of the characters are well-educated, skilled workers at their organization. These factors would indicate that people who may be more receptive to working toward the good of a company, have a relatively strong work ethic, and have a strong allegiance to their specific employer. Many people may work with teams who are composed of less motivated individuals where a strong team is no less important. The team in this story works in careers in which they are passionate and knowledgeable about; some groups may be composed of individuals in a field that they do not enjoy or do not have experience. The executive team in this story often face tense situations that sometimes involve very direct and/or heated conversations. This sometimes resulted in negative responses from the team. A team that may be lacking in the social awareness that is often associated with people who have had more fortunate life experiences or who may be less invested in an organization could result in situations that are much more dramatic. It is common knowledge that most teams function best when there are healthy team relations, but this story does not provide any examples related to dealing with less committed teams. One would need to approach situations of this nature with more sensitivity than when dealing with a team of highly skilled individuals.

Conclusion

The framework provided by Patrick Lencioni in *The Five Dysfunctions of a Team, a Leadership Fable* provide the reader with a clear, well-structured view of what a good team looks like in comparison to a team that is experiencing complications in effective collaboration. Leaders and aspiring leaders can become more familiar with the signs indicating a team becoming recalcitrant and an understanding of the implications of having a dysfunctional team within an organization. The fictional characters and setting will allow readers to experience varying personalities in a series of realistic events. Even with the potential bias of the author due to working with teams of skilled individuals, *The Five Dysfunctions of a Team, a Leadership Fable* the book serves as a good guide and creates reasonable view of how to address certain conflicts within an organization.

References

Lencioni, P. (2002). *The five dysfunctions of a team: A leadership fable.* **San Francisco: Jossey-Bass.**

YOUR KNOWLEDGE HAS VALUE

- We will publish your bachelor's and
  master's thesis, essays and papers

- Your own eBook and book -
  sold worldwide in all relevant shops

- Earn money with each sale

Upload your text at www.GRIN.com
and publish for free